Bishops' Conference of England & Wales

TO BE A PEOPLE OF HOPE

ADULT EDUCATION: A CHRISTIAN PERSPECTIVE

Edited by
A. Patrick Purnell SJ

Blessed those who find their strength in you,
whose hearts are set on pilgrimage (Ps. 84.5)

Published with the authority of the
Department of Christian Doctrine and Formation

COLLINS

ACKNOWLEDGEMENTS

It may be unwise to attempt to compile a list of people who have been involved in the preparation of this document because of the length of time it has taken to produce and the possibility that some may be forgotten and because of the great number of people involved in one way or another in its production. Nevertheless, I feel a need to put some of those names on record in order to offer them my gratitude for the time they have given and the interest which they have shown in its production.

Bishop John Rawsthorne
Sr. Madeline Cecile-Prendergast
Mrs. Jane Collier
Fr. Jim Gallagher
Mr. Arthur Keegan
Miss Angela Lawrence
Mr. Anthony McAffrey
Sr. Anne McDowell
Fr. Peter Wilkinson
Miss Jenny Pate
Miss Clare Thurlby
Fr. John English
Miss Theresa Sallnow
Fr. Jim O'Keefe
Fr. Gerry Murphy
Fr. Andrew Faley
Mr. Chris Harris
Sr. Gemma Brennan
Mr. Michael Brooks
Bishop David Konstant
Fr. Kevin Kelly
Mr. Brian Coxhead
Miss Patricia Jones
Miss Irene Keenaghan
Fr. Brian McEvoy
Mr. Anthony Clarke
Miss Maggie Pickup
Mrs. Sue Chapman
Fr. Joseph Smith
Sr. Margaret Foley
Professor Walter James
Fr. Harry Stratton
Mr. Gerry Capper
Fr. Bill Byrne
Sr. Anne Murphy
Fr. Peter Bristow
Ven. Robin Bennett
Sr. Frances Makower

I further extend my heartfelt thanks to Mgr. Vincent Nichols, the Chairperson of the Bishops' Committee and to its members which supervises the work of the National Project.

Finally my thanks goes to Sister Bernadette O'Donnaghue who typed and re-typed and photo-copied uncomplainingly.

A.P.P.

Living and Sharing our Faith is the title of the **National Project of Catechesis and Religious Education** in England and Wales. The Project takes seriously the shifts of emphasis in catechesis and religious education which are outlined in both Church and educational documents: the stress on the community's responsibility, the pastoral priority of adult education in faith, the need for greater partnership between home, parish and school, the need for clearer understanding of the specific function of each of these settings so that those who live and work in them may perform their own distinctive task with more confidence and at the same time be better able to work with and support each other in their different tasks.

Also available in

Living and Sharing our Faith
A National Project of Catechesis and Religious Education

Our Faith Story A. Patrick Purnell SJ
Guidelines Jim Gallagher SDB
All is Gift: Guidelines for parish catechists working with children Lynn Walker

Contents

Preface

Until relatively recently, though with honourable exceptions, the notion of education has been associated primarily with young people and with *being taught.* This very welcome new work edited by Fr. Purnell shows how much we have changed and how fundamental that change has been in this regard.

The General Catechetical Directory (1971) gave us a very significant nudge when it said that *'catechesis for adults, since it deals with persons who are capable of an adherence that is fully responsible, must be considered the chief form of catechesis. All other forms, which are indeed always necessary, are in some way orientated to it':* a message that was repeated forcefully in Pope John Paul II's Apostolic Exhortation *Catechesi Tradendae* after the Fourth General Assembly of the Synod of Bishops in 1977.

It is probably still true that the most powerful motivation for adult education in the Church in England and Wales is through the needs of our children, with parish based sacramental-programmes its chief focus. But that first taste of working with other adults in this area opens many other doors. Whatever the starting point or motivation, *To be a People of Hope* shows the exciting and challenging world that we are already immersed in and which is the world of the work of the Holy Spirit.

Rather than a book *about* adult education, *To be a People of Hope* invites adult reflection, discussion and response . . . so that it will become necessary to produce another book which in its turn and in accord with the nature of adult education cannot be the definitive one!

Many people have been involved in thinking through and working out the ideas contained in this book. And as Chairman of the Bishops' Committee for Adult Christian Education, I am extremely grateful to them for their contribution and to Father Purnell for coping with the kind of consultation that he himself encouraged at every stage of its production. Finally I would like to stress that *To be a People of Hope* is being offered as a working document which aims at encouraging and stimulating discussion among people about the needs and possibilities of adult education within their own situations.

✠ John Rawsthorne
Chairman
Bishops' Committee for Adult Education

TO BE A PEOPLE OF HOPE

From the very beginning of our existence,
from our first whimpering cries,
we struggle to make sense
of who we are and what we are
and of the strange new furniture of our lives
of sounds and smells, of warmth and cold
of light and shadow, of hands and faces;
to put together
the bits and pieces of our experience
into some kind of order,
into some kind of pattern
so that we may live without fear
in the midst of the powers and the forces
which threaten to overwhelm us.
We cry to one another,
'What have you discovered?
Do you know the way?'
and to those who have gone before,
'Let your light go on burning;
tell us your secrets.
Set out your experiences
in ways we can make our own,'
lest we live as foreigners in the land,
alien to one another's ways,
strangers to the spoken word;
for to be human
is to live in a world of meaning;
but to be without meaning
is to be a stranger
to the human condition.

The setting Who are the adults?

Twentieth century

This book attempts to say something about the theory and practice of adult education. Before setting out into the mainstream of the presentation, we think it worth spending a little while talking about ourselves as adults belonging to the closing years of the twentieth century. What kind of people are we? What kind of society have we made for ourselves? What kind of lives do we lead? What are our values? What dreams do we have for our future?

We are first and foremost inheritors; people with a history. The story of our people goes back into the far distant past where it mixes with the stories of other peoples and other races. Nearly two hundred years ago the pace of human technological progress began to quicken, to run and to race headlong into the middle of the twentieth century. The momentum has continued unabated. Today we can look at the twentieth century in its closing years and know that more has been accomplished on planet earth in this century in the standard of living conditions, in the way people are housed, fed, clothed, travel, communicate, recreate themselves, than the sum total of all that our ancestors accomplished with their science and technology. Now we have the means at our disposal, or at least we have the skills to discover those means, to go a long way towards ridding the world of much of its hunger, diseases and ignorance and setting up a society governed by justice, love and peace.

Yet this is not happening. We have failed to share our technological riches with all the members of the human race. Rich and powerful enclaves have emerged. And so we have failed to make the peoples of the world into one people. We wage war upon one another, kill, maim, reduce towns to rubble and fields to waste lands. We live in a divided world; divided into rich and poor; into hungry and well-fed; powerful and powerless; literate and illiterate; divided into armed camps each protecting its own territory with weapons which could annihilate the very planet itself.

A divided world

We live in a divided world. On the large canvas of the world we customarily speak of a North-South divide polarizing plenty and scarcity, or of the East-West Blocs epitomizing communism and capitalism; but these dramatic opposites penetrate into every crevice of the society in which we ourselves live. On a seventy pence bus ride we move through areas of city deprivation and devastation to well-cared for suburbs of tree-lined roads of houses. The same bus can pass the struggles of a local racially-mixed community for a nursery school and the easy comings and goings of the private school, a mile further along the road. From the bus we can see workers pouring out of a local factory and men and women making their way to the Unemployment Benefit Office.

The setting for adult education

This is the world; this is the setting in which we are to engage ourselves in adult education. We will come to see that the kind of adult education we intend to present has at its heart a mutual sharing of whatever the participants find meaningful and supportive in their lives. This involves sharing knowledge rooted in personal experience; what we struggle to share with one another is personal knowledge, the truth-by-which-we-live. Hence as we open the doors on our presentation of adult education, we find ourselves opening the doors on our own lives. The knowledge which forms the content of this kind of adult education is lived-knowledge, knowledge we have made our own, knowledge which carries with it the experiences which have shaped and given it form; the fruit of personal experience. Such an approach to adult education involves us in trying to understand ourselves as participants in what we will come to speak of as the process of adult education.

The political arena

In attempting to present the participants of adult education in the context of their daily lives we enter the political arena, because politics are about people and about their relationships to one another.

We do not enter this arena objectively, unbiased, as if we did not have a political viewpoint. We enter as christians struggling to make the mind of the gospel our own; and the gospel presents us with criteria, a set of attitudes and a cluster of values which define and characterise our approach to people and to their interpersonal relationships and, therefore, offers us the makings of a political mind-set. The gospel, nevertheless, while setting out ways to help us interpret the world in which we live and make sense of our experiences, is not a party political manifesto. The gospel urges us neither to the Right nor to the Left. What the gospel does is to demand that we treat people, men, women and children, whatever their colour, religion or race, with total respect. It leaves us the freedom to work out how we do this, but the crucifixion warns us not to expect success.

In reading what follows, therefore, we ask you not to be hasty in reducing it to party political terms and then supporting or condemning it. Readers are asked to suspend party political judgements and to read what follows in the light of their own experience of life, thus feeling their way into the process of adult education which works for their enrichment.

Personal stories

Adult education is about people and about how they relate to one another; it is about community and how people in community share with one another whatever is meaningful and supportive in their own lives. Adult education, therefore, attaches great importance to people getting to know one another.

We always need to remind ourselves of the uniqueness of each and every person. Everyone who comes into the process of adult education comes with her/his own unique approach to life – an approach formed and fashioned by their years of growing and maturing; formed and fashioned by race and place of birth, by a particular social, economic and political context, by family relationships which are special to her/him alone, by education, by friendships, by employment, to name but some of the more important factors. Each one comes into the process of adult education with her/his own story to tell.

THE HIGH STREET

We live in towns and villages, in isolated country places and in inner cities, by the sea and on the sides of hills, along wide busy roads and up factory lanes. Sooner or later, we all go shopping and if we want to meet one another, there is no better place than the High Street – any High Street.

Our High Street is the middle of a long road which begins in an industrial estate, moves north-west through terraced houses, sweeps in a long double bend of shops, pubs and banks comprising the commercial sector and then climbs into wooded country where you may catch sight of tailored lawns around well-appointed houses.

In our High Street, the people from down the street leave their private worlds behind net curtains, window boxes and doors which open out on to the pavement to mingle, do business and shop with those who have left their quiet worlds up the hill amid the privacy of the trees. Here in the Street we find one another; the young and the old, the newly-wed and the well-married, faces creased and weary, faces young and full of life; white faces, black faces, brown faces; teenagers after the latest release; mums buying shoes for toddlers; dads buying paint in the DIY; old men hunting a bargain in a sale; the blind with white sticks; the handicapped in wheel chairs; bank clerks, secretaries, doctors, lawyers, cooks, gardeners, motor mechanics, teachers, milkmen, postmen, bookies, stockbrokers, and the unemployed. They are all here in the Street: protestants, catholics, baptists, muslims, methodists, hindus – believers, unbelievers, atheists, agnostics, saints, and villains . . .

HOMES

When we study the society in which we live, we are disturbed by the number of marriages which end in divorce; nevertheless two out of three marriages are working and most divorced people marry again. There is a longing in our hearts to find another person whom we can love completely and who will love us and with whom we can make a lasting relationship. We all want a home. We all need homes.

Into our homes, we welcome people for friendship's sake; we exclude those we do not want to know. Our home is our private world, a sanctuary for ourselves and for our nearest and dearest. Over the threshold, a young couple carry their newly born baby to begin family life; relationships grow deeper and more thoughtful or turn sour, become bitter and dissolve; children grow up loved and cared for or abused, battered and humiliated[1]; the chronically sick and the handicapped are nursed with love and compassion or are ignored, shut away in a corner and treated inhumanly; a teenage delinquent is made to feel one of the family or is turned out of the house; an alcoholic member of the family is tolerated and supported or is excluded and banished; and over the threshold the dead are carried to their graves.

The kind of homes we have or do not have, for we have many homeless people in our midst[2], illustrate perhaps more than anything else, the deep divisions in our society.

[1] *The National Council for One Parent Families estimates that there are about one million one parent families in the United Kingdom, with the care of 1.6 million children.*

[2] *In 1987 there were 100,000 families officially homeless in England alone.*

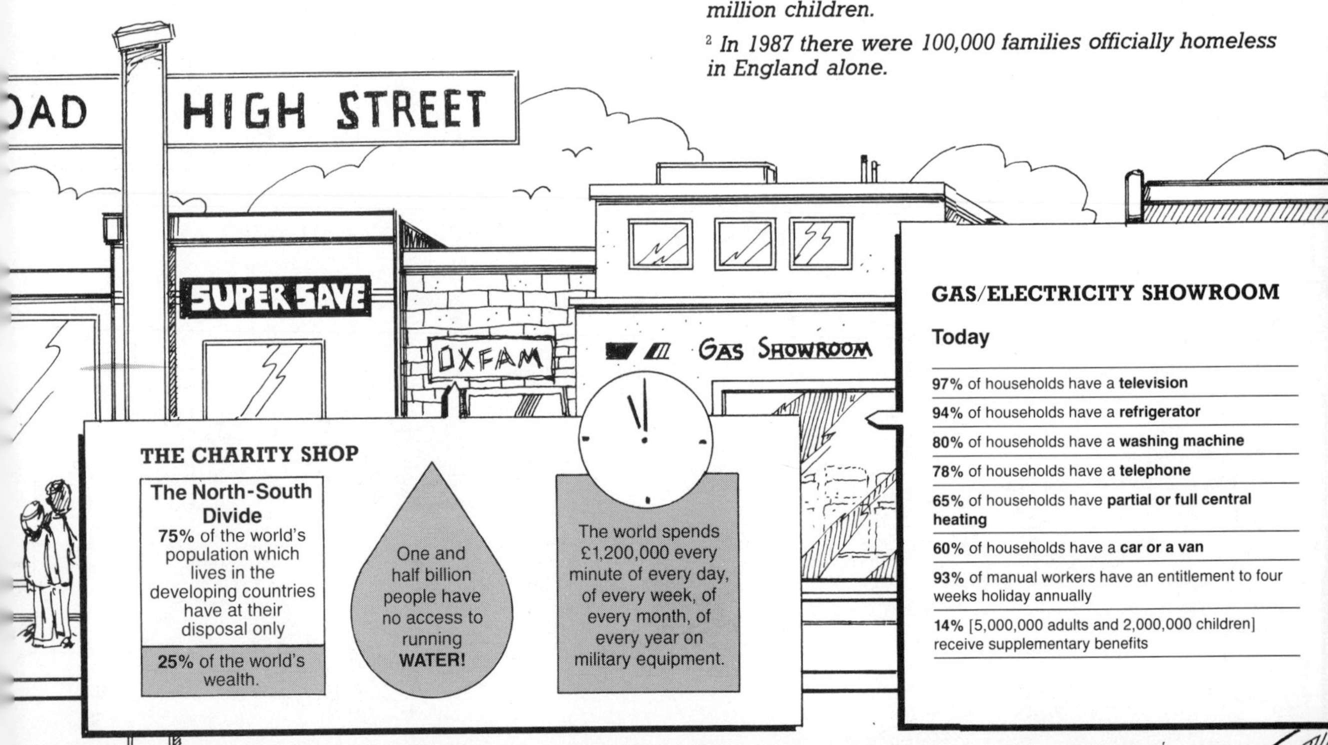

THE CHARITY SHOP

The North-South Divide
75% of the world's population which lives in the developing countries have at their disposal only **25%** of the world's wealth.

One and half billion people have no access to running **WATER!**

The world spends £1,200,000 every minute of every day, of every week, of every month, of every year on military equipment.

GAS/ELECTRICITY SHOWROOM

Today

- **97%** of households have a **television**
- **94%** of households have a **refrigerator**
- **80%** of households have a **washing machine**
- **78%** of households have a **telephone**
- **65%** of households have **partial or full central heating**
- **60%** of households have a **car or a van**
- **93%** of manual workers have an entitlement to four weeks holiday annually
- **14%** [5,000,000 adults and 2,000,000 children] receive supplementary benefits

EXCELSIOR THE SUPER SAVER

Excelsior, the superstore, speaks of many things. It assures us how well off our country really is. It tells how our standard of living continues to rise. It comforts us by implying that there cannot be much wrong with us when we can live like this. It promises a golden future. On the other hand, Excelsior is silent about many things. It does not publicise that department which exists to collect the debts of those who overspend and to repossess the Video they could not really afford. It is quiet about its store detectives who watch for those tempted by the glitter to slip into pockets and roomy shoppers what they cannot pay for, and politely ask them to come to the manager's office. It can take no account of those who weigh the price of everything they pick up lest they top their weekly dole money or their social security benefit. It cannot measure the heartache of those who want so much more than they can afford for their children.

TRENDYFIT

This is where the young buy their gear. For the clever and the astute, the new technology is offering fantastic careers and the ever-expanding service industries are beckoning more and more newcomers; but for nearly a quarter of the young people coming into the job market each year, the prospects are bleak; once they have spent time in some youth scheme, they trickle towards the queue for social security.

Never before have the imaginations of young people growing up been so profoundly activated by, on the one hand, endless possibilities of what life could be all about and what could happen to them in a bright and prosperous future, and on the other hand the possibility of complete annihilation. They hover between a technological utopia and the Waste Land. A recent survey (Gallup mid-year 1986) discovered that four out of ten people under twenty-five thought that life had little meaning for them and less than one in five of their parents thought that their children were happier than they had been.

THE BANK

We live in a capitalist society whose dynamic is personal success. In this society it is assumed without debate that success, marked in terms of the advantages of education, technical skill, professional status, and the power to make decisions, should entitle its holders to a markedly higher income. This makes the bank, whose business is money, par excellence, the symbol of those 'who have made it'.

Its value-system is grounded in what a person has in the bank. Capitalism sets people against people. Competition belongs to its very nature. Theoretically, it respects individual freedom and proclaims the fundamental equality of worth of every member of society. In practice, however, capitalism has great difficulty in incorporating into its structures those who fail and in protecting their freedom, in fact, in understanding freedom in the context of failure. Capitalism can be deeply concerned about poverty and make provision by offering 'charity' and pity to the poor and weak in order to relieve the worst distress and help individuals; it stops short of compassion, because compassion includes a desire to be one with the other, to eliminate what separates.

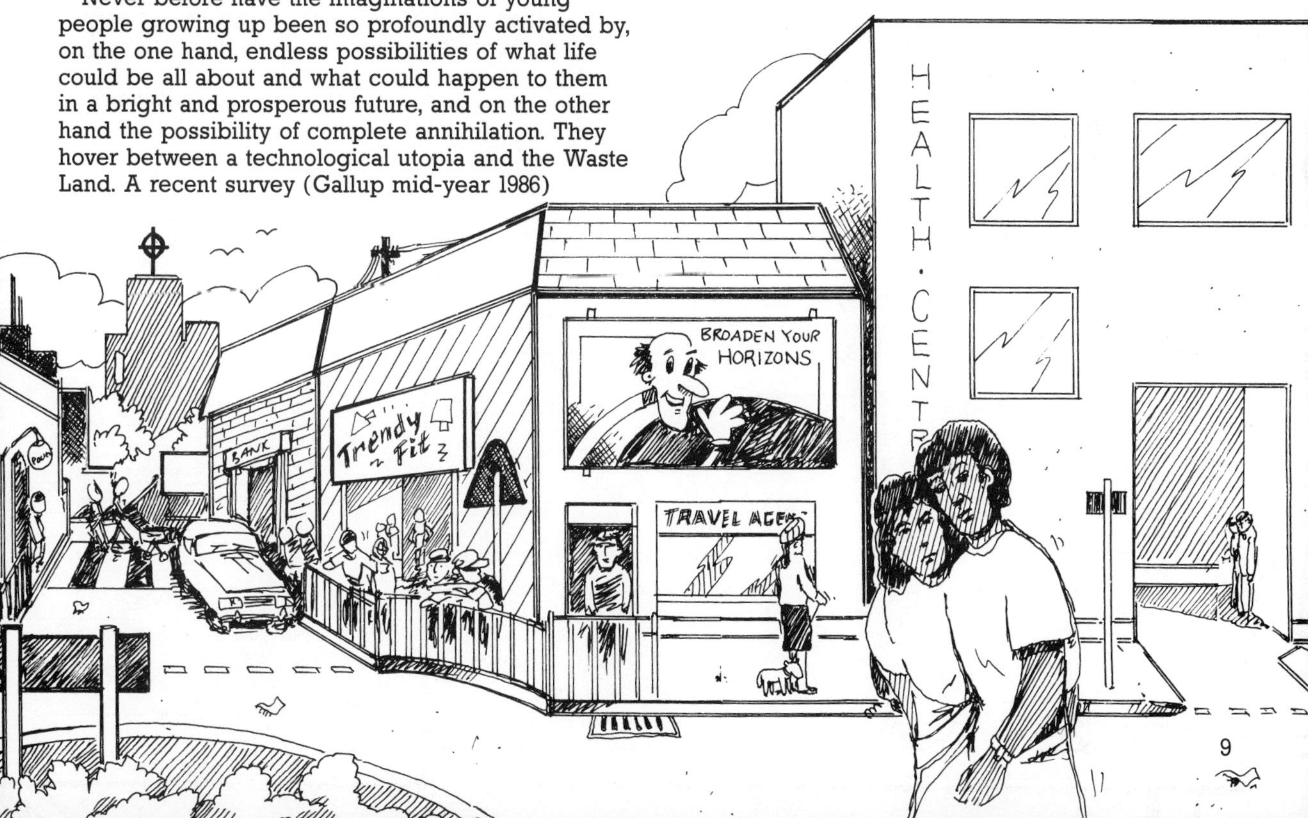

THE HEALTH CENTRE

The Health Centre stands where the old Elementary School once stood. You need time to go to the Health Centre; waiting is the order of the day. Here while you wait you put the neighbourhood and the world to rights; here you pour out your worries and fears, share your hopes and joys and bend your ear to your neighbour's problems.

The doctors are kind and friendly. Each sits in an office and struggles to adjust to each patient as one quickly takes the other's place. Each patient is different; each has her/his own background and circumstances. Each one needs more time than the doctors can give.

Doctors have to deal with as many social and psychological disorders as cases of real medical illness. Again and again they have to be social worker, counsellor or even priest to deal with their patient's guilt. Modern medicine offers many pills to allay symptoms; the temptation is to hand these out rather than work for a cure.

INDIAN TAKE-AWAY

Next door to the charity shop, the Patel family run an Indian 'Take Away'. They have a thriving business.

The presence of the Patel family reminds us that we live in a multi-ethnic and multi-cultural society. People of Indian, Pakistani, Bangladeshi, African, Chinese, West Indian and Arabian ancestry are now an integral part of the population (about 4%). They have brought with them their own rich traditions and customs and ways of worship. There is here a great potential source of new life to enrich British culture. Nevertheless, many white Britons feel threatened by their presence. Eight out of ten people questioned recently (Gallup: mid 1986) thought that racial tension was mounting. In the same poll, 51% said that Blacks and Asians should be encouraged to return to their homes, not heeding the fact that about half the black people living in the country were born here. However, there is some slender evidence that young people are more tolerant of people of other races than their elders.

Black people are more than twice as likely to be in semi-skilled and unskilled jobs as white people, who are more likely to be in skilled and white collar jobs. White people earn on average £20 a week more than black people. Black people are two to three times more likely to be unemployed than white people. They are far more likely to live in the inner cities than whites. In parts of the black communities (West Indians, Bangladeshis) children tend to under-achieve in school. Recent research sponsored by the Department of Education and Science has linked black underachievement and behavioural problems of black children to teachers' attitudes (black children are put on courses and entered for exams lower than their ability warrants). Black people convicted of crimes are more likely to get custodial sentences than white people convicted of the same crime.

THE UNEMPLOYMENT BENEFIT OFFICE [THE U.B.O.]

At the time of writing, just under 3 million of the workforce are officially unemployed and almost half have been unemployed for more than a year.
The U.B.O., therefore, is always full, from the young (25% of the under '25's') to the late middle-aged, men and women, black and white (the proportion of black is significantly higher). Unemployment corrodes the quality of people's lives and brings in its train a litany of financial, domestic, psychological and social problems. Many feel it is their fault that they have no work and this reinforces their sense of inadequacy and powerlessness.

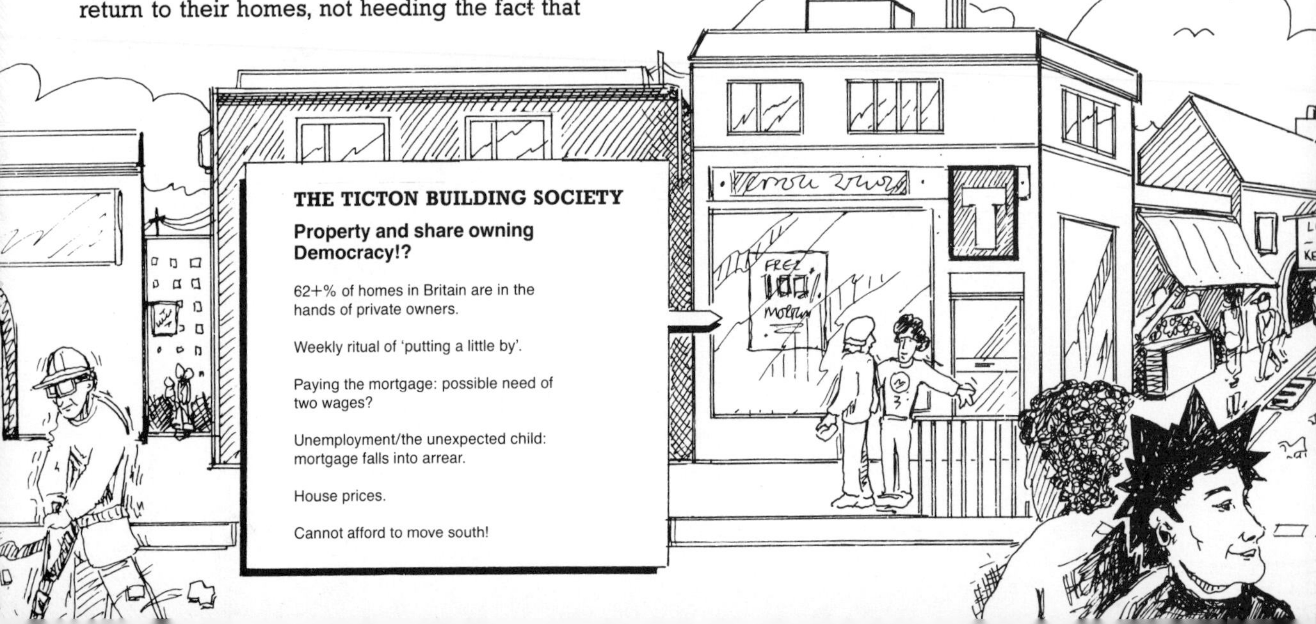

THE TELEVISION AND VIDEO SHOP

For all of us, television is a kind of backdrop against which we lead our lives. Much of it serves as a fairly harmless relaxation not requiring any participatory effort. It can also operate as a powerful stimulus to heighten our perception of people, events and things, to shape the human imagination and to stimulate our desires for the things we see.

'Soap operas' have a magnetic quality about them. The continuing stories, whether they are set amid working class people or among the very wealthy, reflect the stories of those who watch; they draw people, as all good stories do, into the action, and viewers struggle to sort out their own lives as they watch.

The ad-man bombards our senses with the promise of a new tomorrow. For those of us who already feel inadequate, the advertiser reinforces our poor self-image by telling us about all the things which we lack and by suggesting ways of fashioning us to a new image with the help of an ideal diet, the right cream, the potent lotion, and the devastating hair style.

Perhaps more than anything else television implants in our sub-consciousness a certain unease with the reality of daily living, by projecting its own fantasy world into our minds and hearts. In some of us this fantasy translates itself into violence; in others it produces a hankering for what we cannot have, leaving us disillusioned with life.

THE RADIO SHOP

The radio shop sells records and tapes. Surely, music ranks among the most pertinent of the 'signs of our times'. In the last twenty years and more, music has dominated life in a way it has never done before; music from the time of rising to the time of going to bed; music in the superstore, music in the hairdresser, music in the cafe, music in the railway station and music in the airport; slow music, fast music, classical music, jazz, blues, reggae, name a music and you can switch it on and you begin to move to its rhythm. And with this music come endless lyrics which tell the stories of the 'times' and of the people, their searching for love, their playing fast and loose with relationships, their rejection, their loneliness, their enjoyments, their tears and grief, their idealism, their cruelty and viciousness, their powerlessness and their endless selfishness.

THE LION AND KETTLE

The pub is one of the few places where people of diverse backgrounds can meet, talk and reflect upon life. Here in the pub you have a circle of long-standing acquaintances and friends who are your own rather than your family's and whom you would not normally invite home. The pub community can be a true community. A great deal of talking goes on as well as listening. Here, people really express at times genuine concerns about their families, their children and the problems they have to cope with, their jobs and how they get on with people at work, their feelings of pain and disillusionment, their experience of powerlessness and the pain and frustrations of their own lives.

THE START

What we believe — God Creator and Saviour

We are presenting adult education in a christian context. Therefore, what we want to say presupposes a christian theological framework – a particular set of beliefs.

It lies outside the competence of this paper to give a full and completely adequate presentation of the theological themes which are pertinent to and underpin the process of adult education contained in the following pages.

Nevertheless, we feel it is important to indicate briefly what themes have strongly influenced the thinking contained in the process of adult education as we have approached it.

We acknowledge and proclaim God, creator and sustainer of the human race and of the universe, which God has made to be the home of men and women. We confess God to be the source and origin of all reality; the author of beauty, truth, wisdom, justice and love.

Our faith leads us to believe that God dwells deep within the whole of this created reality and within us, both as our creator and as the one who is saving us, that is, as the one who is drawing us to our destiny, a destiny which we can but dimly perceive, yet which somehow or other will gather to a fullness within each one his or her uniqueness as a human being.

Therefore, in spite of human sinfulness, we affirm the radical goodness of this reality and avow that we believe that God is summoning all the pieces of this reality out of its chaos into one cosmic unity.

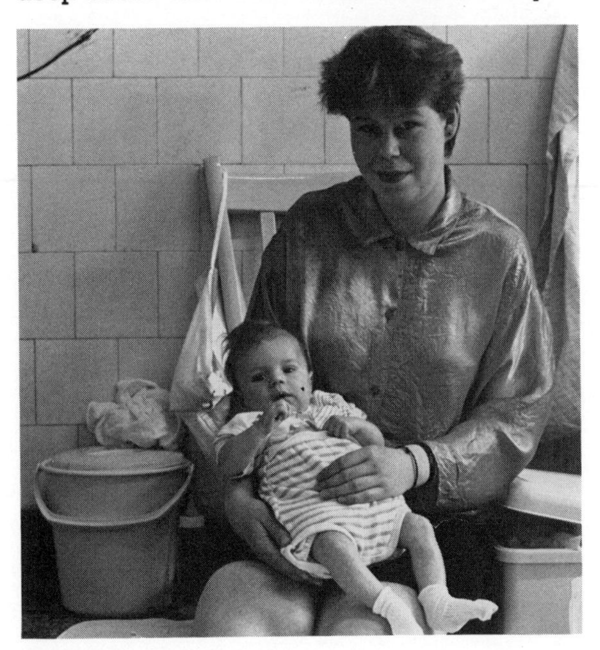

God invites our cooperation in the task of ordering the evolving universe as humankind's home and in the work of achieving our own destiny as human beings. We are called to be co-workers with God to build the evolving cosmos to the pattern of the Kingdom announced by Jesus Christ, the Messiah — the one sent by God to redeem and to re-create the human family.

The Holy Spirit, the Gift of the Father and the Son, calls each person on the face of the earth to know God as Abba and to live together as members of a world family, one world community.

The Church is the emerging model of this community struggling against the powers of darkness to give expression to the oneness of humankind and it is within this unfinished community that we are placing the process of adult education. God's Spirit sets us free for relationship with others; the Spirit within each one is the creative source of our love for, our faith in, our patience with, our care and understanding for, our compassion, sympathy and gentleness towards one another and gives us a desire for the truth and the taste to discern its presence.

GOD'S JUSTICE

Jesus' understanding of God as 'Abba' is at the heart of his relationship to the oppressed and the poor. The Old Testament again and again insists that God is especially present within those who live on the edge of society. Jeremiah thunders against King Jehoiakim for looking after himself and not caring for the poor; he reminds him of how his father had acted justly, *'He used to examine the cases of poor and needy'* and adds that this is what Yahweh demanded, *'Is not that what it means to know me?' (Jer. 22, 13ff.)* When the rich oppress the poor, when merchants give short change or tamper with their weights or follow market economics and put up prices in time of scarcity, when the wealthy make unjust demands in the matter of interest on loans, when judges take bribes, when authority makes unjust laws, the prophets declare that the God of the Covenant is outraged. Amos attacks the rich and the powerful, *'Listen to this, you who crush the needy and reduce the oppressed to nothing, you who say " . . . We can buy up the weak for silver and the poor for a pair of sandals, and even get a price for the sweepings of the wheat", Yahweh has sworn by the pride of Jacob, "Never will I forget anything they have done".'*

God is not neutral. God is on the side of poor and the helpless with a concern to lift them up, and to empower them; to make them equal members of God's community — to give them their humanity. The Gospels echo and affirm the teaching of the Old Testament. *'In truth, I tell you, in so far as you did this to one of these least brothers of mine, you did it to me'* (Matt. 25, 40). Jesus demands that the poor be heard and considered, indeed be given a preferential place in society and, consequently, that economic policies be subordinated to their demands for justice.

QUESTION & REFLECT

★ God is love and is present within everybody as creator and Saviour; how should this affect the way we see people? How is this God in people who kill, maim and assault people?

★ Jesus calls God 'Father'. Would it have been equally true for him to have called God 'Mother'?

★ Many of us have difficulty with the idea of holiness; we associate it with 'churchiness'; yet we are a 'holy people'. What is holiness?

★ A world community! Impossible! Too idealistic! Just look at Northern Ireland, S. Africa, the Lebanon! Is there any evidence that the world is becoming more united?

★ Education brings to fruition people's gifts; it is a process of affirmation, encouragement, sharing and collaboration. Does this tally with your experience?

★ God is not neutral; God is on the side of the poor. How might this challenge the way we live?

★ Granted that economic policies should be subordinated to the demands of justice for the poor, who is to know when such demands have been met?

Each one of us is unique. There is a life-giving tension between our development as unique human beings and as members of the human community. The community is enriched by what is unique in each one and yet we need each other to become our unique selves.

The source of each one's uniqueness is God. God's holiness is a quality of this uniqueness. We need, therefore, always approach one another with a certain reverence recognizing God's holiness touching and transfiguring our neighbour. Tragically, the pressures of modern life tend to place people in ready-made compartments which ignore their uniqueness; they are pushed about by impersonal authority; they are powerless, imprisoned in structures, which diminish their dignity; they live in squalid surroundings; many have no work and each week have to struggle to make ends meet.

Education calls into being what lies hidden within people – brings to fruition people's gifts and talents. Every authentic form of education touches each one in her/his uniqueness; brings into being the special contribution which each one can make to society and which can be made by no one else. Education is a process of affirmation, encouragement, sharing and collaboration.

THE START

What we believe

Jesus Christ

It is to be noted that we are dealing only with certain aspects of christology here – those aspects which are pertinent to the process of adult education. In this context, the development of Jesus' human consciousness is vital, yet even here we can only touch upon the subject.

The incarnate Son of God had to grow to maturity slowly. Jesus is one with us in that as we develop towards maturity stage by stage, so did Jesus; as we are learners all the days of our lives, so was he a learner during his life among us; and as we depend on others to help us learn, so did Jesus. This is the mystery and the challenge of the incarnation.

In the humanity of Jesus we are dealing with nothing less than God; in this lies the uniqueness of the life of Jesus. The truth of the matter is that the mystery of God dwells fully in Jesus Christ, the Word made flesh; it penetrates every aspect of human experience and thereby gives value to what is human no matter how insignificant it may seem to be.

The Father gave us the Word;
the Word is the Father's Son.

The Word became one of us,
completely human,
like us in all things,
but without sin.

His birth was the beginning of his journey through life, the beginning of his growth and development as a human being — the beginning of his life of faith.

Mary and Joseph gave him love and security

so Jesus learnt to appreciate his own value and significance;

Mary and Joseph supported and cared for him

so Jesus came to know that he had within himself the inner strength to cope with his world; he learnt to stand on his own two feet; he gained his own independence and freedom; and was enabled to take responsibility for himself and for the decisions he made.

Mary and Joseph shared with him their belief that good was stronger than evil; that life was more powerful than death

so Jesus learnt to hope and within this hope to fashion a vision of a kingdom which would come in the fullness of God's time.

Jesus grew in wisdom and understanding

Jesus' upbringing was that of a Jewish boy of his day. When he was of age to understand, his parents shared with him the story of their people and of the God they worshipped. They told him about the Law and how it had come down to them, they introduced him to their ways of prayer and worship and Jesus began to seek God in prayer.

During his adolescence Mary and Joseph supported him as he began to examine and question what he had been taught in the course of his religious upbringing. Along with his peers, he searched for a faith which he could really call his own. He shared with other adolescents the struggle to relate the religion he had received with his own experiences of life, love, friendship, personal achievement, hatred, jealousy, beauty, freedom, frustration, hypocrisy, compassion, violence, success, vandalism, happiness, and with what it meant to be poor and powerless in a land controlled by a foreign power.

From his earliest years, from the first beginnings of his self-consciousness, Jesus felt drawn to God and in a world broken and disfigured by sin, he found himself making God's will the touchstone of his life. Jesus lives and dies alongside us so that we might cope with the mystery of God, so much of which lies hidden from us. In his prayer, he came slowly to a deeper and deeper sense of God and at some point in his life came to realise that the nearest human experience to which he could compare his relationship to God was his relationship to Joseph, the man he actually called 'Abba'. God was his 'Abba'! For his time, a revolutionary idea!

The Gospels portray Jesus as one who was totally involved in life. He reflects upon the daily experiences of his life, upon people struggling to make a living, fishing and farming, upon human greed and covetousness, upon the simplicity and joy of children, upon death and childbirth, upon women at work in their homes, upon anger and violence, upon the rich and the powerful, upon the religious leaders and how they conducted themselves: and then he held his experiences up to the mirror of his ever-deepening consciousness of the mystery of God and from out of his inner self he shared with his hearers his perception of the true life. His stories made the people question their understanding of God; his healing ministry spoke of God's fatherly involvement in this world; and his sharp indictment of the self-satisfied hypocrisy of the leaders of his day and the way in which they trampled on the poor and the powerless led him to propose a new vision of society marked by justice and charity.

It is within the life of Jesus that we can see all the strands that make up the process of adult education exemplified. Jesus himself went through the whole business of growing up, developing and maturing;

he was a learner – he learnt from others and from life;

through his understanding of God as Father he totally respected and loved his fellow human beings and came to see how God gave the poor and the powerless a special place in God's kingdom;

prayer as a way of being with the Father was central to his life: on the one hand, in prayer he found the Father in an intimacy which we can only imagine, while on the other hand, there were occasions when we can see him sharing our lot of struggling with God's silence and apparent absence.

And all the time, he was empowering others, simply by being with them, to be of service to their fellow human beings.

STORY

Stories are accounts of experiences either real or imaginary.
Stories have meaning: they are, therefore, a way of helping us understand our lives.

Everybody has a story to tell

We can tell stories about where we were born, about how we grew up, about our parents and the different members of our family; about all the people who influenced us in one way or another – our teachers and our friends and, indeed, our enemies; about our first job, our first love, our marriage or entry into religious life or ordination, the birth of our children, buying a house, losing our job; some of them will be happy stories; some sad; some about success and some about pain and frustration.

Everybody has a story to be heard

The way to understand people is through their stories. The stories of other people help us to find a way into their lives, and their stories help us to understand better the story we ourselves can tell. Through our stories we are helped towards friendship and together we are drawn into community.

We are all story tellers: we tell stories about ourselves: about our families: about our friends: about the place we live: about the community to which we belong: about the country in which we live.

God is always present in our lives:
When we tell stories we are saying something about this God, living, loving and at work within us – saving us.
God is at the very heart of the experiences we weave into stories.

QUESTION & REFLECT

★ Mary and Joseph helped Jesus grow up into a mature human being. What light does this throw upon your understanding of Jesus and upon our need of one another in our attempts to become mature adults?

★ Mary and Joseph loved one another and gave Jesus an environment of adult love. Mary and Joseph loved Jesus and this love gave Jesus a sense of his own value and significance. Why is it important to have a real sense of one's own significance? What happens to an individual who has no sense of her/his own worth?

★ We believe that good is stronger than evil and that life overcomes death. How did we come to have these beliefs? How did our parents and other important adults in our lives help us to believe these things? Can all parents help their children to believe?

★ God is Abba! Is this your image of God?

★ What was the last story you heard about somebody? How do stories help us to understand our lives?

Description of adult education

Everybody is a learner

One of the most important elements which runs through this presentation of the process of adult education is that everybody has a contribution to make to the process and everybody is a learner. When we say 'everybody', we indeed mean 'everybody' from, for example, the learned professor to the 'unlearned' individual attending her/his lecture.

The professor brings her/his experience and learning with her/him into the process; the one who comes 'to learn from' her/him brings her/his experiences of life along with what knowledge she/he may have. What we are saying is that the process demands that the professor respects and explores the contribution of the 'pupil' as much as the 'pupil' aims at making her/his own what the professor contributes; and, furthermore, the 'pupil' is enabled by the support and the respect incorporated in the process to get in touch with the unique contribution which she/he can make.

The objection may well be put that this approach undermines what many have always considered essential to teaching, that is, the handing on of a body of knowledge, complete and intact. It might be suggested that the process being proposed here could lead to everything being uncertain and relative. Not so; the process, on the one hand, asserts that what is being handed on is a living body of truth, not an inert body of knowledge and, on the other hand, that each discipline has its own norms of discerning whether what is being treated of remains true to its original insights. In handing on the christian story, as we shall see, the process, while giving due respect to the riches of experience and activity of the Spirit, embodies particular norms for discernment, namely, scripture, the way the Church worships, the teachings of the Church and the way that christians have given witness to the gospel in their lives.

QUESTION & REFLECT

★ Do you think it is important to make sense of our lives? Why?

★ Do you think those without faith can make sense of their lives?

★ Journeying involves searching. We are all on a journey; we are all searching. What are we searching for? Does the idea of the 'search' help or worry you? Do you think that somebody actually has the answers?

★ Can you remember the things you thought important when you were a teenager or a young person? What do you think you then wanted out of life? In what ways have these changed?

★ Does your faith help you to make sense of your life? What does this mean to you? Do you feel you can share this faith with others? What help would you need to share it?

★ Why is hope so important? Have you ever lost hope? What experience caused it? What do you hope for? for your friends? for your family? for those you do not like?

★ What would you like to change in yourself? in others? in the neighbourhood? in the world? Do you think Christians are called to change society?

★ People's needs get adult education going. What are your needs? What do you think the people closest to you need?

What is adult education?

Adult education is the deliberate and intentional interaction which takes place between adults on their journey of life.

This interaction presupposes and involves a personal (dynamic) relationship between adults in which they attempt to meet the needs of one another.

This they do by sharing together, formally and informally, whatever is meaningful and supportive in their own lives so that they may be of service and value to one another with the purpose of exploring together the meaning of God's kingdom of truth, love, justice and peace and of advancing its coming.

Meeting one another's needs

Adults meeting the needs of adults. We use the plural to emphasise the creativeness of people meeting people; the group/the community has a power of its own.

It is the needs of people which gets the process of adult education started. It is not a question of some adults deciding what their fellow human beings should know; it begins in our being sensitive to and discovering our own needs and those of others and entering together into a search for the good, the beautiful and the true. We use our skills to make it possible for all of us to share what is within us and thus we empower one another to grow and mature.

Meaningful and supportive

We share what is meaningful and supportive.

Meaningful is the truth and the values by which we live and which help us to make sense of ourselves, our personal relationships and the world in which we live. We share with others the personal knowledge gained from reflecting on our experience of life; our truth and the values which flow from it – the truth-by-which-we-live. Facts, information about life, are the raw material which we fashion; we make it our own truth – truth to be shared. Granted all this, there is, nevertheless, because of the mystery which shrouds our lives, much which remains without meaning and, indeed, appears absurd and contradicts the possibility of a loving God; it is precisely here that we need the support of one another in order to be able to live with these contradictions and absurdities.

There is a degree of hesitancy in the way we offer the truth-by-which-we-live. We have no way of determining beforehand whether other people will attach the same importance to it as we do. We offer it tentatively, giving the other the space and freedom to think differently.

Supportive: crucial to our relationships with others is concern and compassion. We want to build up our fellow human beings to have a true understanding and appreciation of their intrinsic value, and to have the confidence to stand on their own two feet and play their part in this process of adult education.

Risk of sharing

There is always a risk in sharing the truth-by-which-we-live. We have to be ready to be challenged. People may even ridicule our truth and our values. This may lead us to reassess, perhaps to deepen what we believe, or to discover another way of presenting our truth.

Kingdom of God

The Kingdom of God is a symbol for what is not yet but is hoped and longed for. It offers a vision of a transformed society – of a new world. Adult education equips us to become involved in working to make the world a better place in which to live. The Kingdom vision helps us to look at our own lives and the society in which we live in a new way; we begin to ask questions about the very kind of society in which we live and why things should be as they are. We look for radical alternatives as real possibilities and examine ways in which we might become involved in bringing them about.

The aim of adult education is to set people free

AT A PERSONAL LEVEL

THE AIM OF ADULT EDUCATION
is to empower us
as individuals and as members of our communities
to take charge of our personal lives
and play a responsible role in the life of our communities.
so that we may be able to make decisions for ourselves
and have a part in the decision making process of the community.

Adult education empowers us
Empowering is the gospel work of Jesus. Jesus heals us in order to set us free from everything which undermines our personal freedom; the blind see, the deaf hear, the cripples walk – signifying the recovery and redemption of people's spiritual powers to see what Jesus is doing and what he stands for and to hear from him the words of life and so to enter into companionship with him.

Jesus releases in us as individuals and as members of our community the power to be of service to others and to give prophetic witness to the kingdom. We are empowered to give sight and hearing to one another, to enable our neighbour to walk, in a word to set people free: free from ignorance, prejudice, and all those unreasonable pressures which breed superstition, inhibitions, and a false self-consciousness which prevents us from owning our lives as individuals and as members of community.

QUESTION & REFLECT

★ Do you ever say to yourself, 'I feel trapped.' What do you mean? Do you really feel that you are in charge of your own life? What are the kind of things that seem to limit your freedom? To what are you enslaved?

★ 'I never felt freer than when I was in jail.' What do you think he meant?

★ 'My family is both my source of freedom and my prison.' How can this be?

★ Can you think of people whom you simply want to tell what to do? How does one set about helping people to stand on their own feet?

★ Hope separates the free from the slave. Why is hope an essential part of being human?

★ The death of hope is the birth of despair. What is the difference between depression and despair?

★ Is the death and resurrection of Jesus the source of hope for you? Why?

THE AIM OF ADULT EDUCATION

is to set us free
as individuals and members of community
so that together
we can order our lives
according to the vision
which the Kingdom puts before us.

INNER STRENGTH

Adult education sets people free from believing that life is too much for them. It is concerned with us helping each other to realise that we have within ourselves the inner strength to cope with life. It is the Holy Spirit who invests our spirit with the inner strength to grow and mature and bear the difficulties and problems of life; it is the same Spirit who is the creative cause of our ability to help one another, for the Spirit is the source of the attractiveness by which we are drawn towards one another. Moreover the community in helping us to love and esteem ourselves provides us with the support to stand on our own two feet and live through the conflicts and tensions which arise in our lives.

SELF IMAGE

Adult education sets people free from a false self-consciousness, a sense of inferiority, a poor self-image. It helps a person learn to appreciate her/his qualities and abilities and thus begin to own her/his life and take her/his rightful place in community.

Injustice lies at the heart of the way our society is organised; some benefit from its structures while others suffer. The success ethic announces that everyone who tries can get on in life, and those who don't are worthless and inferior. As a result of this way of thinking, the poor, the disadvantaged and the powerless feel shame and lose their self-respect. The unemployed, for example, are led to believe that anyone who tries can get work and so better themselves. They come to think that being unemployed is a reflection on themselves. In this and other ways many become trapped in feelings of inferiority.

True freedom requires a true love of self. God in creating shares God's love with the work of God's hands. We are loved into existence and because we are loved simply for what we are and not for what we do we are loveable.
A good self image begins to emerge when people are affirmed, accepted and acknowledged as of significance even (and perhaps especially) when they exhibit their ignorance and weakness and share their fears and limitations with us in community.

A paradox! Frequently we feel overwhelmed and crushed by events and people; we feel powerless and, yet, somehow in that feeling of disenchantment a new and deeper kind of life emerges.

HOPE

Adult education sets people free from despair. It offers hope without which a truly human life cannot emerge. Many people feel that there is a disastrous inevitability about the forces unleashed in the world; it must all end in some terrible calamity. They feel, too, that they are getting nowhere; they have no sense of achievement.

- Parents struggling to understand their growing teenage children;
- workers being challenged by new technology, which threatens to change their familiar patterns of work;
- young people fearing nuclear annihilation;
- unemployed people nursing frustration and helplessness drifting into apathy;

all see the future not as something in which they can fulfil themselves but as a danger which might engulf them. They feel powerless: there is nothing they can do; they feel victims of fate.

Christians express this hope in terms of the kingdom of God and in their belief in the Passover Mystery of death and resurrection, which is confirmed in the risen Christ of whom they are the Body.

Education proclaims the hope that humankind can make progress to a better life.

Hope believes that good is more powerful than evil; that life is stronger than death.

Hope is rooted in God's loving care for us and that this love gives us an intrinsic value and dignity.

Hope professes that we can grow and develop and become that which God desires us to be — fully human.

Hope gives us the courage to accept the struggle involved in growing and developing and the readiness to pay the price in acknowledging and integrating our shadow side.

Hope separates the free from slaves.

Hope enables people to set goals.

The aim of adult education is to set people free

AT A STRUCTURAL LEVEL

Adult education sets people free from the very structures of society in which they live.

Every society has structures, laws, political, economic and social systems. Born into a society, we simply take these structures for granted: we don't question them. When we speak of freedom, we rarely mean anything other than freedom within these accepted structures.

If, for example, we speak of the rights and the freedom of workers, we do so within the accepted economic system; seldom do we question whether the system itself may be unjust.

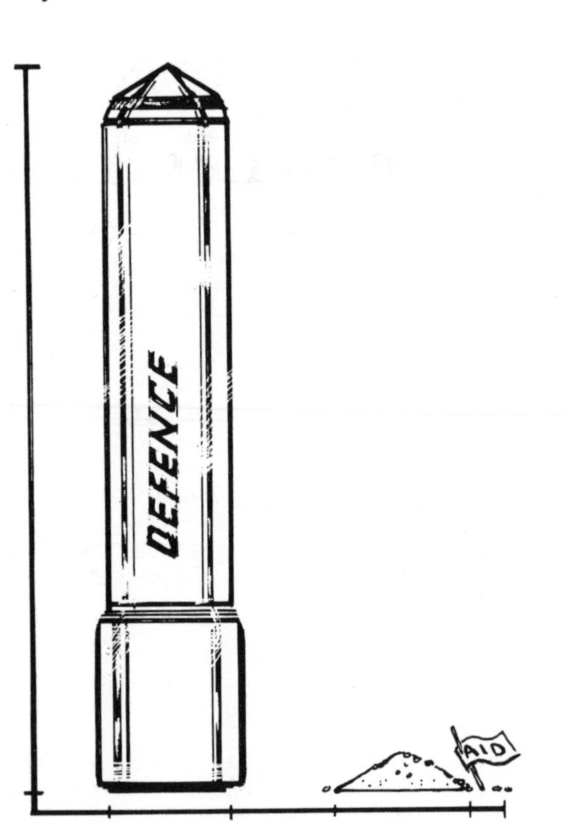

**Historically, slavery was once an integral part of the economic structure of society — the New Testament encouraged good relations between masters and slaves, but did not question the structure of slavery itself.*

**During the persecution of the Jews in the Concentration Camps, the Commandants defended themselves by saying they were only obeying orders.*

**Pilots dropping napalm during the Vietnam War declared, 'I only pressed the button'.*

It is extremely difficult to question the social, economic and political structures of one's own country. For example, in Britain today, the structures which oppress black people demand to be questioned: economically they have more difficulty in getting work than any other sector of society; politically they have little voice; and socially and educationally they achieve less in society's terms. The black community is dominated by the institutional racism and vested interests of white people's power structures.

Similarly economic and social structures and the organisation of the church discriminate unjustly against women.

There are many other groups who also feel unjustly discriminated against: for example, married couples feel the tax laws are unjust; travelling people feel ostracised at many levels; the divorced feel discriminated against by the church; single parent families feel economically disadvantaged . . . and so on.

Adult education sets people free from believing that there is nothing they can do about the structures which govern their lives.

** It shows people a way of getting in touch with the historical dimensions of a given situation for example, the North-South divide in Britain or the origins of economic policies which cause imbalance of trade between the First, Second and Third Worlds. It tries to enable people to tackle structures which appear to have a permanent, immutable quality, shored up by vested interests that resist change.

** It offers people a way of reflecting on the society in which they live. It looks at our society in its diverse parts, economic, political and cultural, considering race, sex, class, ethnicity, religion, geography etc, and looks also at its place in the international world in order to try to understand exactly for whose advantage this particular society functions and who are its victims. Thus it enables people to ask the kind of questions which reveal where power and self-interest really lie and what effect this has on the poor, the underprivileged and the powerless. It enables people to consider what implications this has for their personal and communal actions.

** It tries to help people take into account the long term consequences of what they are doing and of what is happening in society in the present, and to use this insight to evaluate what is presently happening.

QUESTION & REFLECT

★ Do you agree that society discriminates against women: as persons? in family situations? in work situations? in retirement? Is this also true of the church?

★ Together in a group, can you itemise some of the things which we take for granted as part of life and which we feel can never change?

★ Talk over together the statement, 'Everybody is a racist'. How racist are you? In what ways does this show itself? Is there a difference between racism and prejudice?

★ Can you give examples of self-interest at work in society as a whole today, and in your immediate experience? Does what I do as an individual count for anything?

★ Do you believe that we can behave today in such a way that our behaviour will shape the world for the next ten or twenty years?

The aim of adult education is to set people free

AT A SOCIAL AND CULTURAL LEVEL

Adult education sets people free from those obstacles which prevent people from attempting to meet one another's needs. *The heart of adult education is sharing with one another whatever is meaningful and supportive in our own lives.* This is often made very difficult by the social and cultural forces which govern our relationships. Adult education helps us to evaluate our approaches and attitudes to one another.

FIRSTLY, we know it is almost impossible to appreciate the needs of others as vividly as our own. We live within our own world: this we know; here we have our bearings.

The more different another's world is, the less real will her/his needs be. Adult education helps us face this difficulty and offers us tools to enter other people's worlds, to learn compassion and to appreciate their richness. It shows us a way of standing in another person's shoes.

SECONDLY, we all tend to divide others into *people like us and other people.* With people like us, we share the same interests, have the same values; we believe that our interests are indisputably unbiased, irrefutable, balanced and identified with the common good; whereas those of others are unreasonable, selfish and destructive of what is best in society and for society.

Adult education helps us to see that these clashes of interest are not easily or normally resolved through moral persuasion or reasoned argument. It offers another dimension; there can be no resolution of rival positions except through the desire of the participants to be of service and value to one another.

People like us?

Whose power?

THIRDLY, adult education helps us to understand the part which power plays in our society. Prestige accompanied by power is a dominant factor in human culture.

Power assumes many forms, from the naked desire to dominate or to protect a vested interest at all costs, to the more subtle kind where we gain prestige and hence power for ourselves in working selflessly for others. Moreover, in attempting to share what is meaningful and supportive in our lives, we can be tempted to want those with whom we are sharing to fall under our influence. All power does indeed corrupt!

FOURTHLY, adult education helps us to understand where the power lies in the systems which we use in everyday life.

For example much of the planning for future change is done in committees, and the professionals who know how to handle committees and who have the skill to present facts and figures to support their views will readily outmanoeuvre the lay person. It is sometimes said that those who make the agenda, rule the world.

FIFTHLY, adult education helps us to understand powerlessness. Power implies the ability to change ourselves and our situation, to influence people and events; it implies the ability to make choices and come to decisions as to what to eat, what to work at, where to live etc.; it involves the possibility of taking responsibility for others and working for their good.

Power enhances us with the capacity to give and this capacity to give is the source of our self-respect and dignity.

Powerlessness, therefore, implies no freedom of choice, no possibility of responsibility, no share in decision making and no capacity to give.

QUESTION & REFLECT

★ What do we mean by compassion? Do you agree that it is important in adult education?

★ The more different a person is the more difficult it is to understand that person. Why?

★ Can you give your own examples of what one means by 'people like us'? What are the qualities of 'people like us' and the qualities of 'the others'?

★ Rival positions cannot generally be resolved simply by reasoned arguments; what more is needed?

★ What kind of power do you already have? Who is in your power? Whose power are you in? What kind of power would you like? What would you do with it?

★ 'Real power lies with those who can work the system'. Have you had any experience of this?

★ Power involves the ability to make choices. Where do you feel you are powerless?

★ The capacity to give is a source of self-respect. Do you agree?

New Horizons

Education for change

EDUCATION IS ABOUT CHANGE

Education is about change

- about changing people – about changing the way we think and the way we act;
- about moving the world in a new direction.

We live in hope: hope for a better future – a more compassionate, a more just society, where people live together in peace, truth and love, caring for one another and sharing the goods of the earth, and in which no one section of society dominates another, and no one country imposes itself on another.

We feel overwhelmed by the proportions of the task.

The present state of affairs is shored up by super powers and multi-national companies, secured by the vested interests of the rich and the powerful.

What can we do? In what direction should we be struggling to achieve change?

We come together dreaming of a better future, to share our dreams and our hopes and our desires for a better world. We share with one another what is meaningful in our lives; we offer one another our support. We slowly become community; and as community, we become a rich resource; we begin to see many different possible ways in which we can go together into the future. As individuals we find in community power to change ourselves and as we change so the community becomes an agent of change – of transforming society.

RENEWAL OF THE CHURCH

The Church is God's gift to the world. When we talk about transforming society, we must include the renewal of the Church.

The Church is made up of ourselves, human beings continually in need of being redeemed and made whole.

It is a mistake to think of the renewal of the Church as something apart from the transformation of ourselves and the society in which we live. If we think of Church renewal as something separate, then the Church can become almost exclusively parochial; the local parish community can become engrossed in altering the liturgy, setting up prayer groups, moving the altar and the statues, totally oblivious of the needs of the people in the neighbourhood, the lonely and the depressed, young families struggling to 'make a go of it', single parent families, families with juvenile delinquents, the neglected old.

EVOLVING VISION

Growth and development

Our personal growth and development is about maturing and fulfilling ourselves as human beings. Our creator made us human. Jesus, God's Son, is the clearest statement about what it means to be human.

This growth and development is more than a question of fashioning our private and hidden selves, it involves also our growth and development as members of a community. We need one another in order to mature.

But our growth and development also hinges on our commitment to bringing about the Kingdom – to transforming society and renewing the face of earth. Therefore our growth and development as human beings involves us as political instruments for change.

Challenge

For some the call to transform society will come as a challenge, calling them to give of their best.

For others it may be an obstacle to what they see as the 'true' religion.

Adult education must challenge; it must make demands on our potentialities; it must offer possibilities; it must put before us *new horizons;* it must extend and deepen our vision, our hopes and our dreams.

However we are not called upon to go it alone. The transformation of society is to be the work of the whole community; it is a community enterprise.

We are involved in a process; the process of adult education.

Process is about growth and development and here we are talking about our own growth and development; what is involved, however, in the process of adult education is our conversion – indeed our veritable transformation.

Now process, as such, can be a very messy affair because our growth and development as individuals and as communities is not usually a very neat and ordered exercise. We are often faced with ambiguity and doubt; we have to struggle with forces which are hostile to our humanity; what we experience can, at times, appear utterly meaningless.

The process gets under way because we have some vision of where we want to go — we have a goal.

We use gospel language to describe this goal. We talk about bringing into being the Kingdom of God without knowing exactly what this means.

It follows that we cannot be absolutely clear about what happens on the journey to that goal; the goal is not fixed and final.

Nevertheless there is always sufficient vision, sufficient light, sufficient insight into the future to move the process forward; sufficient to offer us hope that the way will continue to become clearer as we journey on.

We have to be content to live in the provisional; to proceed into the future step by step. It is by reflecting on each step and sharing together what we think that we discover our way forward.

QUESTION & REFLECT

★ Have you ever felt so strongly about a situation that you had to become involved (e.g. housing, education)?

★ Some people argue that education is to prepare people to live in society as it is; others argue that education is about change — about moving the world in a new direction. What do you think?

★ Unless a people dreams, there is no future for society. Do you think this is true? What are your dreams?

★ Christians must be involved in transforming themselves and society. Individual salvation is tied up with the salvation of the community. Do you think this is the message of our parishes?

★ What are the forces we discover within ourselves which are hostile?

★ What experiences do you have of the Church as excessively parochial?

New Horizons

Politics

Politics are about how society functions. It is about how a particular society works; about the course it is taking; about the future of different policies and where the society is heading; politics analyses what might be wrong with a society and what needs to be done to put it right.

Because society is such a complex network of relationships and interlocking systems and structures, there is no easy answer to any of these questions; all we can do is to develop theories and compare one with another; try them out in practice; see which one is more suited to this or that situation and which one works.

Hence we have a multiplicity of political ideologies which vary from the extreme Right to the extreme Left.

A political ideology is made up of ideas, beliefs and attitudes, out of which it aims at trying

- to make its own sense of past experience,
- to grapple with present problems,
- to relate different parts of humankind's store of knowledge to improving society's future or some particular vested interest within that society,
- and to struggle to produce policies to put into practice.

THE KINGDOM

The Kingdom of God is a symbol of our hopes and desires. Its fulness belongs to a future reality. We are charged to inaugurate it in our present world. We have to work to make it effective, not only in our own personal lives but in our communities and in the society of which we are part.

When we move from the personal and in-house dimension of our calling as christians to the society in which we live and its structures, we move into the political arena. We have to examine the invisible web of relationships which holds society together and which we take so much for granted that we cannot readily imagine a different order of things.

We may have to face the fact that the structures which provide us with comfort, security and an abundance of material things may be the cause of injustice to another sector of society. One person's riches may be and often is the cause of another's poverty. Our privileges may cost other people's suffering.

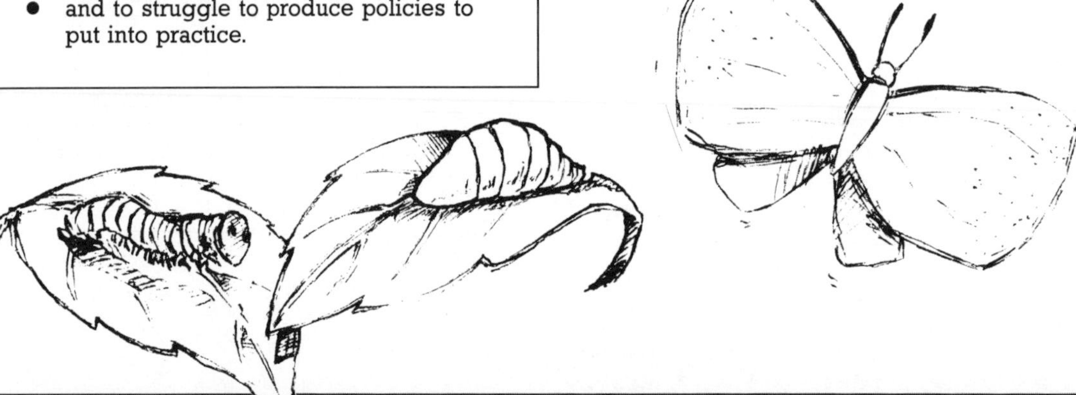

Adult education is about change – about the transformation of society. Change takes us into politics. Adult education is a political tool.

NEW HORIZONS

Adult education is concerned with personal growth and development; with everything that the gospels portray as authentically human.

To live in a truly human way is

- to live in relationships with our fellow human beings
- to be open continuously to the effects which these relationships can bring about in us
- to be aware of the effects which we have on others.

It is the experience of these relationships, their complexity and richness and the conflicts which they engender, which deepens our understanding of the nature, the context and the quality of life — of what it means to be truly human.
People being involved with people empower one another

- to take charge of their own lives,
- to make their own decisions,
- to play a responsible role in their community and their society.

Something new begins to emerge

- the new self
- the new community.

The challenge of the Gospel begins to make itself heard.

CONFLICT AND UNITY

It is a serious misconception to believe that we can grow and develop either as individuals or as members of church communities or as members of society by fudging issues or denying that they exist for the sake of peace and quiet. To deny conflict undermines the validity of the process of adult education which brings together a vast diversity of human beings with their own presuppositions and different ways of thinking and styles of living.

QUESTION & REFLECT

★ Why do politicians tell the Church to stay out of politics?

★ Adult Education is a political tool. Should we, as Christians, become involved in politics (i) in the broad sense? (ii) by joining a particular political party?

★ A person has a right in justice to make as much money as she/he wants as long as she/he keeps the law. Do you agree?

★ The only way in which we can attain true justice is in and through community. Does this mean that everyone must be equal?

★ Conflict is an essential part of growth and development. Can you share experiences of healthy conflict? When is conflict destructive in the family? at work? in the parish?
Are there times when conflict cannot be avoided?

Unity is not a characteristic of the provisional nature of our present reality nor of the journey we are making. Gospel unity always has a hope-filled dimension about it; unity belongs to the goal of the journey not to the journey itself.

Conflict is part and parcel of all human relationships.

Conflict arises from the clash of self interest whether of individuals or of the community or of different sections of society.

Conflict is also part of the process of growth and development as it meets resistance from the status quo. It is creative; it is a necessary part of human growth and development.

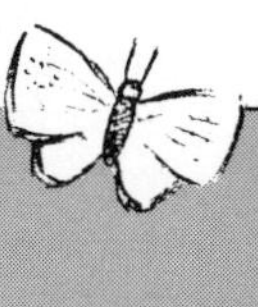

Adult education aims at helping us live within the conflicts and tensions of life; it helps us to understand our experiences of turmoil in the light of the gospel and to find within the very struggle the hope and the life we seek.

OURSELVES

We who take part in adult education

What we bring to adult education

Each one of us enters into the process of adult education as teacher and as learner.

We bring ourselves to the process and the process is about sharing our experiences with one another.

We have, therefore, to become aware of what we ourselves bring to the process; what we ourselves have to offer to other people.

When we begin we may not be able to do this very easily. Part of the fruit of being in touch with other people is to realise what lies within ourselves. Often this is a long slow business: we have to learn how we are affected by our own culture,

- how we are influenced by tradition
- and how this tradition sets up within us certain presuppositions.

We slowly discover what exactly we do know, and what skills we have.

We come to know how we are influenced by fears, prejudices, likes and dislikes, what our limitations and our strengths are, how vulnerable we are and how we are held by the political, economic and social structures of our society.

Neutrality

We don't have to be neutral. Neutrality is not a virtue we need to acquire. Certainly in those issues which touch us most deeply – issues which stem from our commitment to the gospel – we cannot be neutral. We enter the process as christians trying to understand and live out our commitment to Christ.

What is important is that we know that we are not neutral and acknowledge the influences which play a decisive part in our lives.

We must also expect that as we continue to become more and more involved in the process we may come to understand those influences better and in a new light. We need to remember that what is happening in ourselves is also happening in the lives of the people we are sharing with.

Willing victims

Experience tells us that some people are only too willing to be told what to think and what to do and what to believe. Bad adult education can be responsible for reinforcing this view; a dominant personality can ride rough shod over people; can deceive her/himself into believing that she/he knows what is best for the other.

Frequently the willingness to be subject is caused by a loss of self-worth, a poor self-image; a person has been so ground down by the events of life that she/he is willing and content to be subject to others.

Adult education is a way of love; the 'willing victims' can be transformed by love; unless you are loved you cannot stand up and take control of your own life.

The fruits of adult education

The results of this kind of adult education emerge slowly, though one of the results is the actual involvement in the process itself. The results cannot be foretold in advance. When we share what is meaningful and supportive in our lives, this will not necessarily have the same effect on others as it has had in our own lives. We cannot forecast what effect it will have.

QUESTION & REFLECT

★ Each of us is both a learner and a teacher. Does this alter your views of education?

★ There is nobody who is not biased about something. What is your bias?

★ What is the difference between being neutral and respecting what another person believes or doesn't believe?

★ Why cannot Christians be completely neutral?

★ How would you set about helping another person discover her/his skills?

★ Surely it is a good thing to bestow the benefits of western civilisation on others. We are helping people become less primitive. What do you think of this statement?

★ Do we take it for granted that everybody sees God the way we do?

★ 'Imposing our God on others': do we tend to do this with children?

★ Have you ever learnt something about God from your children?

★ Have you ever listened to a handicapped person speaking about how others see him or her?

★ Some people simply want to be told. Have you experience of this? How do you react to it?

DISTORTED ADULT EDUCATION

Adult education can become distorted when one set of people enters the process believing that it is superior to the other. Historically we have examples of this in the relationship between conquerors and vanquished, where the former attempts to impose a culture on the latter. Slavery and apartheid are the direct effects of the white conquest of Africa and S. America. The whites assumed the role of saviours to rescue the ignorant and depraved. The conquerors believed that they were benefitting the inhabitants of those lands by bestowing on them the fruits of an advanced civilisation.

The God of the victors

The missioners who accompanied the conquerors set out to uproot every vestige of paganism; they cleared the lands of idols; they began the task of conversion to the 'true God'.

No matter how sincere the missionaries were, no matter how much they loved the people of the land they had invaded, the people had become a conquered people; what they were being offered was the 'God of the conquerors'. What kind of God was this, who allowed them to become a subject people?

Assumptions of the victor

There was no sharing between the victors and the conquered. No consideration was given to the kind of society in which the inhabitants lived – it was simply assumed by the victors that their way of life was better and that everything they brought with them would benefit those they had conquered. The missioners did not believe that they had anything to learn about God from their 'subjects'. Today, missionaries try to understand the way God lives in people of cultures alien to their own: they enter into dialogue with people of other faiths.

Echoes of this distortion, however, continue to appear in the relationship between authority in its many different forms and those under them.

Compassion • Insertion

ENTERING ANOTHER'S SITUATION

At the heart of adult education lie the relationships between those taking part and central to these relationships are the ideas of insertion and compassion.

Insertion

The word 'insertion' arises out of our understanding of the Incarnation; the Word became flesh out of compassionate love for us and inserted the divine self into our humanity, so that we might come to understand the nature of God's total commitment to humankind from the very first beginnings of creation; and in order that we might appreciate more clearly God's invitation to us to share in the divine life. The idea of 'insertion' has, therefore, something to say to us about how we become involved in one another's lives, about how we make ourselves one with others and their situations. It means that we acknowledge our responsibility as a member of the human family, for our part in the making of the other's situation. We come to see that our own story meets their stories and that their stories become parts of our own.

Compassion

Compassion is a quality of this insertion; compassion draws us to people; it is the way in which we become involved in the lives of others – the way we come to understand that 'No man is an island'.

We are involved with people through a whole complex network of relationships, some of which are absolutely necessary in order to make life possible, tolerable and secure, while other parts of this network can be the source of grave social injustice.

In some situations we are *directly* involved through an active participation; in others, *indirectly,* through our passive acceptance of the structures and policies of the society to which we belong:

- the nature and network of family relationships;
- the education system;
- the prevalent economic system;
- the judiciary;
- the political system;
- the defence policy;
- the health system;
- the church's teaching and ways of worship and government.

Compassion makes us sensitive to the contributions which people make to each other's lives, and to the price which some people have to pay for the security of others.

Distorted consequences

Some people are unemployed and suffer the ills of depression and loss of self-esteem because of a particular economic policy.

For some, family life destroys them as persons, instead of offering them the security in which to grow and develop.

Again some people end up resentful and bitter because they feel themselves unjustly and harshly treated by the law.

Yet again some may feel rejected by the Church because, for example, of the Church's attitudes to marriage.

> The price that these people pay could be a complete mistrust of any kind of authority, an inability to make close personal relationships, a poor self-image, a desire to exact vengeance, a terrifying legalistic approach to life, an image of an angry God.

The image of an angry God or a God indifferent to human misfortune lies deep within the lives of many people overcome by misfortune: they may for example be victims of

- cruel family misfortune, perhaps physical or mental abuse in childhood
- bad religious education
- an unhappy marriage
- racial intolerance
- loss of religious freedom
- mental or physical handicap

All these things could lead a person to a very distorted concept of God.

Compassion means trying to enter into these different situations, trying to make the sufferer's stories our own, acknowledging that we might have some responsibility for what they suffer, or seeking some role to play in alleviating their suffering and preventing similar situations in the future.

QUESTION & REFLECT

★ Adult education involves us in other peoples lives. Why?

★ Compassion makes us sensitive to the price which some people have to pay for the security of others.

★ What in your experience gave you an understanding of compassion?

★ Does suffering change people: yourself? a friend?

★ How has becoming involved in a friend's life changed your own? How has it had an effect on the decisions you wanted to make?

★ How can family life destroy people?

★ God is sometimes presented as supporting the status quo. How would this affect a black person's image of God?

★ Have you ever had an image of an angry or legalistic God? How did the image arise, do you think? How did you work through it?

★ Could the Church's approach to worship produce a false image of God?

★ Have you had any experience of bad religious education? What would you say are the characteristics of good religious education?

Being alongside

Companions

The process of adult education is a journey. 'Being alongside' expresses something of the companionship involved in adult education. We journey together; we accompany one another.

That having been said, we also have to remember that one of the fruits of adult education is to learn how to accompany one another as together we struggle towards maturity and freedom.

Involved in 'being alongside' is knowing where we are on the journey and knowing where our foot will next fall. We come to 'own our lives'. A person who owns her/his life is one who has the maturity to make decisions in the light of the goals of her/his journey; who knows what she/he is doing and where she/he is going, having taken into account possible alternatives and discerned the best way for her/himself. Jesus says of himself, 'I know where I have come from and where I am going' (Jn. 8,4. See also Jn. 13,3 seq.).

Standing in the shoes of another

As we accompany one another, so we learn about one another: how mature we are, how we handle relationships, how we take on board experiences of life and how we interpret them; thus we become sensitive to one another's values, prejudices, fears, likes and dislikes, hurts, inadequacies, powerlessness, ability to perceive and relate one's experiences to one another, desires and ambitions. It is in this way that we can begin to 'stand in one another's shoes'. This first and foremost calls for love, especially when our companions represent ideas, ideals and interests in conflict with our own; this demands of us a certain stripping of the self – a prerequisite for discovery, growth and friendship.

Other people's Gods

On occasion in the process of adult education we will meet people with ideas, ideals and interests very different, even alien, to our own; this encounter presents us with a challenge. It is then we have to remember that the object of 'being alongside' another and entering into her/his life is never to destroy what we find.

In encountering the 'gods' of other nations, the object is never to destroy them but rather to see those 'gods' as part of humankind's search for the 'ground of all reality'; they are milestones on the journey and they must be respected.

'Being alongside' one another means accepting one another as *who* we are and *where* we are and *as* we are with all the luggage we carry, 'strange gods' and all.

'Being alongside' is a question of affirming one another, listening to one another's stories and in so doing coming to understand our own story better, recognizing that we are on a journey together, helping one another see where we have come from and plotting the next stage together. We will find ourselves challenged, questioning begins again and our search is given a new impetus as we struggle to be of help to the one with whom we are alongside on the journey.

Sharing our story in this context, offering the other what we find meaningful and supportive can be a very frustrating and painful exercise. We profess that what we find meaningful and supportive is rooted in the gospel. The very process of sharing this means that we have to clarify constantly exactly what we do believe and purge it of elements gathered from other sources. Again and again we will find ourselves rethinking our own deeply held beliefs and values. This may be very disturbing to us and we will need to be supported as we reassess what we believe and value.

Learning

Enabling learning

Some of us believe that we are incapable of learning; we have no confidence in ourselves. Unhappy and unsatisfactory memories of classrooms drive from us any desire to try to begin learning again. We all need to be helped to believe in ourselves in order to come to recognize and value our gifts. This we must do for one another. The ability to learn is given to everyone; together we have to discover the stimulus to become involved.

Being open to learning

Learning takes place for people in different ways. For some the very fact of sharing is the time when they learn. For others the sharing provides material; they take it on board, go away and mull over it and it will only be activated when the right experience comes along to trigger it off.

There are certain experiences which open us to learning in a way that others do not: the birth of a child, marriage, death, an unexpected happiness, an encounter with pain. They are key moments because they carry with them depths of great feeling and offer opportunities for a new understanding of life. We need to return to them again and again and share them with others, if we can, in order to discover all they are saying to us.

Being open to learning is closely linked to where and how it takes place. Memories of drab classrooms and uncomfortable desks inhibit us.

If real sharing is to happen, the environment must help us to enjoy one another's company. We have to be free to be ourselves. Commonplace practicalities necessary to help people relax must be thought out, from coffee to easy chairs. What we are trying to do is to provide a situation in which we can be comfortable enough to ask questions, to betray our ignorance, to reveal our weaknesses and to feel safe to meet the challenges which sharing may entail.

QUESTION & REFLECT

★ At the very centre of adult education is the ability to stand in the shoes of another. Why?

★ How can we learn from people with very different ideas and ideals to our own?

★ It is never a question of just destroying the 'gods' of others no matter how false they may appear to us but seeing these 'gods' as part of the common search for the true God. How could this apply to our situations? Could it apply to our treatment of teenagers?

★ St Paul says: 'Love is patient, love is kind . . .'; what place has patience in my life with a teenager? In a teenager's life with me?

★ How does the 'success ethic' in modern society distort our values?

★ Struggling to share what we believe with others means that we often have to reassess what we believe. Have you had experience of this?

★ Can you name a key experience in your life which was an important moment for learning?

★ How and when do you best learn?

Process (1)

Process

Learning is the result of the way people act, reflect and interact among themselves. We call this interaction 'process'.

The go-between Spirit

In christian language this *'process' is the setting for the action of the Holy Spirit* – the Befriending Spirit, the Go-Between Spirit.

It is the Spirit who gives us to one another and helps us to be present to one another in order that we may become aware of one another and understand one another.

Community

The process takes place in community. Every member of the community has her/his own story and the community itself has its history – its story.

The community – the church – has a structure, with an authority of its own which is responsible that the story remain true to its original insights; this story provides the criterion or touchstone for the process. Its bishops could be thought of as Keepers of the Story.

Experience is the heart of adult education

Human experience is the very stuff of adult education; and adult education continues to be good adult education in so far as it is rooted in human experience. When we begin to feel we are losing contact with one another we may well ask questions about what we are doing and how we are sharing our life experiences; if the answer is that we are not, then we will not be doing adult education.

Experience

Experience is our relationship to our environment. We could define ourselves as the sum total of all that goes on between ourselves and our environment: the complex totality of all our relationships with our own selves, others, society and the universe.

Everything we do and everything which happens to us becomes our experience as we reflect upon it: everything we see, hear, smell, touch, taste, feel:

it may be an experience of hunger or of being well-fed, of an evening sunset in all its beauty, of being cold-shouldered in a pub, of loneliness or despair, of comfort and happiness, of ignorance and powerlessness, or of wielding power.

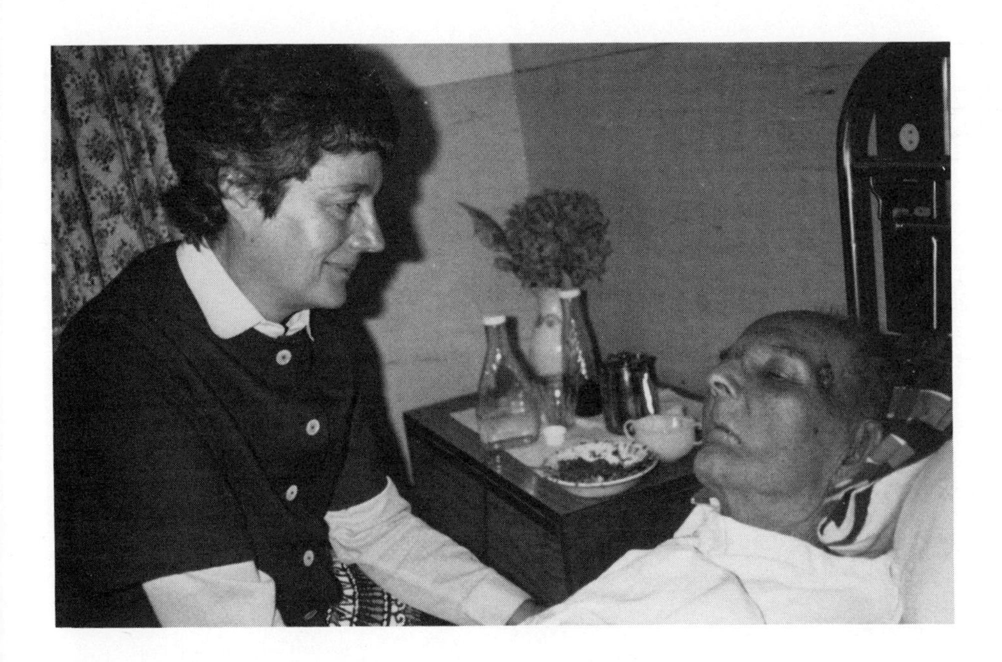

The skill of dealing with experience

When we do something or something happens to us:

firstly, we make it our own: we acknowledge it as our experience;

secondly, we reflect on it so that we may come to understand it and make it part of our lives;

thirdly, in trying to understand it we look at it in the light of the whole of our lives, in the light of our previous experiences; in this way we will begin to see its significance, its meaning and how it may be a source of growth towards maturity or a cause of our diminishment or a challenge which calls us to change and play our part in helping to make the world a better place.

QUESTION & REFLECT

- ★ Can you identify in your own life some experience which has changed your outlook?
- ★ Recall some simple experience; share it with your neighbour. What light does the sharing throw on the experience?
- ★ Now listen to your neighbour's experience. Does it help you to understand your neighbour better? How? Does hearing that experience have echoes in your own life?
- ★ Have you someone in your life whom you can talk to easily about how you feel in yourself? Is the person the same sex as yourself or the opposite?
- ★ What kinds of experience cause diminishment?
- ★ Losing touch with experience makes adult education simply an intellectual exercise. Adult education is much more. How?
- ★ Why do you think the community is so important in adult education?

Process (2)

Adult education helps us to attain the **skill of reflecting and acting up on experiences.**

We need people to help us deal with our experiences. We need one another to make sense of our experiences, to discover within them the presence and action of the Holy Spirit.

People encourage us to reflect because of our need to name what has been happening to us in order to communicate with them. It is in the process of reflection and articulation that we come to see the meaning of the experience and how it may enrich our lives or diminish them: scales may fall from our eyes and we may be enabled to view other experiences in a new light.

People help us to see our experiences not as isolated units but as part of the flow and pattern of our lives: the light of our understanding of previous experiences helps us to interpret new experiences.

People share their experiences with us. We listen to their experiences and the stories they tell about themselves, their families, their friendships, their difficulties and their problems; and we hold up our own experiences to the light of these stories and how the tellers of these stories have understood them.

We need to listen with care and with love; to become one with the storyteller; to get under her/his skin, stand in her/his shoes. This can be very difficult when we are trying to hear someone from a very different background to our own; yet it is imperative that we do listen, especially to the poor and the powerless, because they have privileged access to the Kingdom, its meaning and its values.

Together with other people we need to look at the **context** of our lives and see how this sheds light on how we live and what we experience and how that influences the way we make sense of our experiences.

By context we mean the society in which we live, its history and traditions, its structures and systems, its culture etc. These are all the factors which we take so much for granted and which condition our lives and the meaning we give to our experiences. We must be in a continual dialogue with this context, questioning issues of justice and asking radical questions.

We need to reflect together as a community on the political, social, economic and cultural factors which govern our lives and see in what way we are determined by them.

Next we reflect upon our experiences in the **light of the christian story** and see what light this casts upon them and how it helps us to make sense of what is happening to us.

Finally, with other people we must look at the goal of our lives, **our vision of what life is all about;** this affects the way we understand our experiences and how we make sense of life.

When we examine our experiences to discover what meaning they have for us, we do so

1 in the light of where we have come from – the light of our past experiences; we do this with the help of other people who share their understanding of life with us;

2 in the light of the society in which we live – its systems, structures, cultures, etc.;

3 in the light of the christian story

4 in the light of where we are going – our goal, our vision.

The christian community story is the criterion of the whole process; it is the touchstone which guides the way we make sense of our experiences.

The christian story is contained in

scripture

the way the Church worships

the teachings of the Church

the witness that fellow christians have given to the Gospel in their lives: that is, the way they have made sense of their lives; with them we experience a genuine solidarity.

God dwells in the whole of creation and through it reveals God's self. God makes God's self known in and through the human story. The stories of people tell God's story. God makes God's self known in and through the ordinary experiences of everyday life — in the stories which people tell of what happens to them.

We tend to put God on a different plane — put God out of reach; sometimes we are more comfortable with a God at arms' length. Yet God has shown us in Jesus that God has broken down all barriers. Jesus reveals how God has made God's self totally involved with our world and how we can discover God within our ordinary everyday experiences.

QUESTION & REFLECT

★ We should be ready to tell our own story. Make a list of as many people as you can think of in the whole of your life; people you liked and disliked. Think of the effect they had on you, sometimes for good while sometimes not so good. How have they helped you to make sense of your life? What have the people you disliked taught you?

★ As we listen to one another's stories, so the community story begins to emerge; the story of the neighbourhood; the story of the parish. How have we been affected by these larger stories?

★ Discuss together the statement, 'When we listen to one another's stories, we are listening to how God is active in our world. Through stories we learn more about God.'

★ Have you ever listened to the stories of people of other faiths? Can we learn about God from their stories?

★ Have you ever listened to a young person who feels rejected? to an alcoholic in distress? to the husband and wife in a divorce?

★ Have you noticed any changes in yourself as a result of your listening?

★ To understand stories properly and our own, in particular, we need to look at those things which we simply take for granted and never question; we need to know how we are affected by social and political structures; if we don't we may not really get in touch with the meaning of life. Talk about this together.

★ To discover the meaning of our experiences we must look not simply at what is happening in our lives now but at how we are affected by our goal. Can you put your goal in life into words?

★ What is the christian story? How does it help us to discover meaning in our lives?

The process of adult education

SHARING EXPERIENCE

Each one brings her/his own experiences and story into the process.

○

THE INTERPLAY OF EXPERIENCES

Between present experiences and stories and the story of the community – what has been handed down: the traditions.

○

THE INTERACTION

Between the community and society: its structures and systems.

Between the present and the future – the vision which draws us onwards.

FIRST MOVEMENT
Experience

We bring our experiences to one another. We talk. We listen to one another tell of looking after a sick mother, being unemployed, trying to pass an exam, losing one's temper. We encourage and support one another as each speaks.

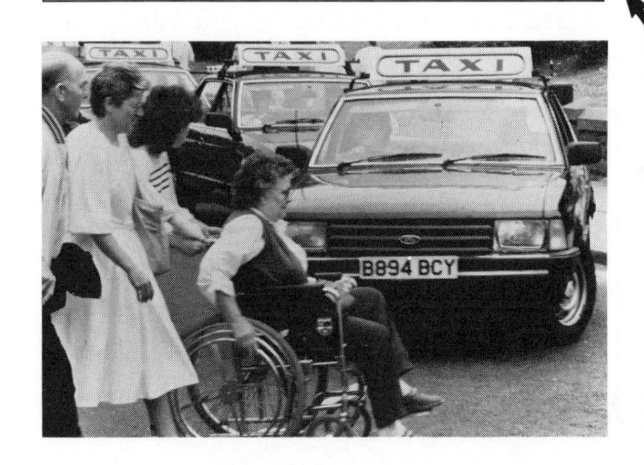

SECOND MOVEMENT
Sharing experience

We try to come to a deeper understanding of what we hear. We talk; we reflect; we listen; we share. We ask questions; how does it feel to be unemployed? to be divorced? How does this experience fit into the rest of one's life? What light does other people's experience throw on one's own? Are there special problems looking after a sick person today? What makes it specially difficult for black people in society today? We try to analyse what is happening? What systems and structures govern our lives. Who benefits from the present state of affairs? Where is the power?

THIRD MOVEMENT
Reflecting and analysing experience

What light does the Gospel throw on what is happening in our lives? We begin to hold up our experiences to the light of Gospels and reflect. We share with one another what scripture puts into our hearts. How does the Gospel challenge us? We pray together.

FOURTH MOVEMENT
Assimilating experience

We begin to make our own what has been happening among us. How does the fruit of our reflections fit into our lives? How does our past experience shape what has been shared among us? How do our hopes shape it? What does the vision of the kingdom make of our present experiences? What meaning is beginning to emerge?

FIFTH MOVEMENT
Action: Looking for a way ahead

We look at the new understanding which is beginning to emerge and ask ourselves how this will affect our lives. What does it mean? What will it entail our doing? What decisions have we got to make? Is it a question of renewing an old commitment in a new way? What new questions does it raise? What are the experiences which will take us back into the first movement?

Search • Dialogue • Commitment

SEARCH

All our lives *we struggle to make sense of our lives:*

we are searchers for meaning – for truth; for the truth; for truth by which to live.

We find fragments as we journey on: our hold of truth is limited and partial but enough to help us see the steps ahead – enough to keep us from faltering on our journey.

We share with those alongside us what we ourselves have gleaned *and listen* to how they understand the truth with respect and reverence.

Together!
We need one another on our journey; we need community to support and encourage us never to give up the search.

DIALOGUE

We need to speak to one another of what we have discovered. We have to find words – a language with which to communicate what lies deep within us; to express what is dearest and closest to our hearts.

We need ears to hear what the other is saying to us – to listen with a profound attentiveness to our neighbour as she/he struggles to offer us what lies within her/him, lest we lose the nuances of her/his words.

To do this with integrity we need to be sensitive to the context of the other's life – we need to put on the other's shoes and walk a mile or two with her/him; we must have some feeling for her/his background, history, tradition, culture, presuppositions, fears.

So we hold up the truth-by-which-we-live to the light of the truth-by-which-our neighbour-lives so that together we may explore the meaning of reality.

We need to share our understanding of truth even when it radically differs from others. It will always be so among us with such a variety of upbringings, so many different cultures and traditions, such a myriad of hopes and dreams and fears.

We have to allow different and contrary ways of understanding to coexist because it is precisely within these tensions, if we hold them with love and respect for one another, that a kind of resolution emerges and then we can see our way forward together.

Yet we need time to reflect and to ponder in order to test within our own truth what we have heard, so that we may come to see what we may make our own.

The end of dialogue is not an agreed statement but a coming together of mind and heart – a willingness to go together into the future searching and exploring.

COMMITMENT

We travel, we journey to satisfy our restless hearts. Searching takes us into dialogue and out of dialogue emerges truth-by-which-to-live.

Dialogue frets away at what separates us from one another.

Truth emerges from the process of people struggling to be one with one another – struggling to be community.

The more the journeyer becomes one with her/his fellow pilgrims, the deeper becomes her/his understanding of life and its meaning.

Truth is alive within us and within our relationships to one another.

Truth grows out of our relationships with one another and it is in doing the truth that we discover what it is.

If you make my word your home, you will indeed be my disciples; you will come to know the truth, and the truth will make you free. (John 8, 31-32.)

If we say that we share in God's life while we are living in darkness, we are lying, because we are not living the truth. (1 John 1, 6.)

Collins Liturgical Publications
8 Grafton Street, London W1X 3LA

Collins Liturgical in the USA
Icehouse One – 401, 151 Union Street
San Francisco, CA 94111-1299

Distributed in Ireland by
Educational Company of Ireland
21 Talbot Street, Dublin 1

Collins Liturgical Australia
Box 316, Blackburn, Victoria 3130

Collins Liturgical New Zealand
PO Box 1, Auckland

ISBN 0 00 599047 5

First published 1987

Nihil obstat Vincent Nichols *Censor deputatus*
Imprimatur Rt Rev Gerald Mahon MHM
Westminster 4 August 1987

The Nihil obstat and Imprimatur are a declaration that a book or pamphlet is considered to be free from doctrinal or moral error. It is not implied that those who have granted the Nihil obstat and Imprimatur agree with the contents, opinions or statements expressed.

CREDITS
Photos
Neil Beer: pp 15, 18, 22, 34 (left), 35, 44, 45, 47
S. Chapman: pp 38, 40, 41
Heinrich Kunkel: p 14
Carlos Reyes: pp 7, 12, 16, 17, 20, 21, 34 (right), 36, 37, 39

Cartoons: Neil Beer

Cover design: Malcolm Harvey Young

Typographical design by Neil Beer
Typeset by Swains (Glasgow) Limited
Printed in Great Britain by Bell and Bain Ltd., Glasgow